LIVING BEYOND DIAGNOSIS

Mission: To Proclaim Transformation and Truth
Publisher: Transformed Publishing, Cocoa, FL
Website: www.transformedpublishing.com
Email: transformedpublishing@gmail.com

All cover, interior, and accent images were retrieved by the publisher, via paid subscription / terms of use from Storyblocks. Copilot utilized for editing.

This work is based on the author's research, life experiences, and personal study. The intention of the author is to share his knowledge, experience, insight, and strategies that have helped him and others through mentorship.

Any resemblance to someone else's life experiences, teaching, actual events or locales or persons, living or dead, is entirely coincidental.

ISBN: 978-1-953241-93-1 (paperback)
ISBN: 978-1-953241-94-8 (hardcover)
ISBN: 978-1-953241-95-5 (ebook)

LIVING BEYOND DIAGNOSIS

How Diagnosis Programming™ Has You Stuck

WILLIAM SCOTT FAULKNER

DEDICATION

I would like to dedicate this book to all the coaches, teammates, psychiatrists, influencers, and pastors who have made an impact in my life.

To coach Al Werneke (God rest his soul), Coach Dale Mays, Coach Nick Saban, Coach Kirby Smart, and Coach Dabo Swinney.

Special shout out to teammates Gerald White, Anthony Mitchell, and Michael Cadore. Football Goats, Tom Brady, Tim Tebow, and my favorite cornerback Ronde Barber.

A special lifesaving head nod to Psychiatrist Earl Taitt who taught me that my diagnosis was not my identity.

To Mel Robbins, Cody Sanchez, Simon Sinek, Jay Shetty, Emma Grede, Oprah

Winfrey, Steven Bartlett and Matthew McConaughey.

To pastors Dr. Bill Faulkner, Sarah Jakes Roberts, Steven Furtick, T.D. Jakes and Andy Stanley.

And I, of course, give the biggest dedication to my parents, Bill and Brenda Faulkner. The most amazing and patient parents of all time.

Without the support, prayers, encouragement, and inspiration of all the beautiful people mentioned, this book would not have been possible.

You all have a special place in my story of learning how to live Beyond my Diagnosis and labels. It is all about setting the standard, walking through the process, and daily choosing to acknowledge that my identity is found in my personal relationship with Jesus Christ.

Thank you all!

TABLE OF CONTENTS

1
The Awakening

"You can't get where you want to go until
you decide who you want to be."
— Nick Saban[1]

I was born in Orlando in June of 1965, long before seat belts were required, but life had already buckled me in for a ride I never saw coming. My childhood unfolded in the shadow of Southern Baptist Ministry, a world where faith was public, image was currency, and the minister's family was always "on display".

My parents were good people, talented singers devoted to their calling, but ministry life meant constant movement. New churches, new towns, new expectations.

Sometimes we moved twice in a single year. I attended a ninth-grade center and then three different high schools. Every move meant another round of the same performance: smile, behave, impress, repeat.

I didn't know it then, but I was learning how to be who people needed me to be, *not* who I was. I was learning the art of the mask; the earliest seeds of what I would later call Diagnosis Programming™.

The Performance Years

Every time my dad interviewed "in view of a call", our family was part of the audition. I was groomed to be the kind of kid a church wanted to hire along with their new minister.

"Yes ma'am."

"No sir."

Smile.

Sit still.

Don't be the weak link.

It wasn't malicious. It was survival. But it taught me something dangerous: If you perform well enough, people will accept you, even if the performance isn't real.

Church kids were easy to befriend because our parents already approved of each other. Athletes were my other tribe. I started playing football in third grade and quickly discovered that speed, strength, and grit earned respect faster than manners ever could. I lived for competition. I lived for the field.

Football became my identity.

Girls came second.

Friends third.

Church and God somewhere after that.

I didn't realize it then, but I was already building a life on two unstable foundations: external validation and raw talent.

The Dream

By high school, I was obsessed with football and track. I studied the game, watched Alabama religiously, and dreamed of wearing crimson one day. Teachers quietly hoped football would carry me to college because academics certainly wouldn't. I wasn't lazy. I was terrified. Books, notes, comprehension; none of it made sense to me. I didn't know how to learn, so I avoided anything that exposed that weakness.

But football? Football made sense. Football made me somebody.

I earned a full scholarship to Austin Peay State University. But instead of stepping onto the field, I was redshirted. The coaches saw potential. I saw failure. I had never missed a game since third grade unless I was injured. Sitting on the sidelines felt like suffocating.

And then came the letter from Alabama.

Coach Al Godwin wrote, "Scott, you have the ability to play defensive back for the Tide. But if you want to play here, you'll have to prove it in the classroom." The one place I had never been.

I remember sitting alone in the rain on the empty field that night, holding that letter, realizing the lights were going out on my dream. I wasn't just losing football; I was losing the identity I had built my entire life around.

The Collapse

I left school. I went home. I married young. I tried to bury the grief. But grief doesn't bury, it ferments. It becomes pressure. And pressure eventually explodes.

On January 28, 1986, I watched the Challenger explode. A moment that shook the nation and shattered my career at the

Space Center. Another dream gone. Another identity stripped away.

I tried to rebuild. I worked at the courthouse. I pretended I was fine. But inside, something was unraveling. The storm I had been outrunning finally caught me.

One night, without warning, I snapped. I screamed. I smashed pictures. I walked barefoot through broken glass. I terrified the woman I loved.

Fifteen minutes of rage destroyed my marriage and changed the trajectory of my life.

The Diagnosis

Years later, after more chaos, more broken relationships, and more self-destruction, I was Baker Acted and diagnosed as bipolar.

In 1993, bipolar disorder wasn't understood. It wasn't treatable. It wasn't manageable. It was a life sentence. At least that's what I believed. And once I believed it, I lived it.

This was my first experience with Diagnosis Programming™. The moment when a label becomes a script, and the script becomes your identity.

I became the stereotype. I became the warning label. I became the thing people feared. And I believed I had no control.

The Wilderness Years

I spiraled.

Drugs. Sex. Violence. Gangs. Sixty jobs. Three marriages. Three daughters I lost connection with. A grandson I held once. A trail of wreckage I didn't know how to repair.

But even in the darkest years, something in me refused to die. A spark. A whisper. A question, *What if this isn't who I am? What if this is who I've been conditioned to be?*

The Turning Point

Six years ago, everything changed. I met a psychiatrist who didn't treat me like a diagnosis. He treated me like a human being. He didn't just medicate me; he taught me how to think. How to slow down. How to question my reactions. How to interrupt the storm.

He taught me the foundation of what would become my life's work: The Elite Mindset™. Diagnosis Programming™. The Walk-about™. The Reframe. Living Beyond Diagnosis.

For the first time in my life, I learned that mental struggle is not always mental illness. And a diagnosis is not destiny.

I learned to press pause. To identify triggers. To reframe my response. To walk myself out of the storm instead of being swallowed by it.

And for the last five years, I have experienced long stretches of stability, not perfection.

The Truth: The Diagnosis Didn't Disappear

This part matters. I am not cured. I am not "fixed". I am not free from the diagnosis. I still take medication. I still have ups and downs. I still have days when the storm clouds gather.

But here is the difference: I no longer live according to the identity inside the diagnosis. I don't wake up expecting chaos. I don't assume I'm broken. I don't let the label tell me who I am.

The struggle is real, but so is the strength. The diagnosis is real, but so is the discipline. The symptoms are real, but so is the strategy.

And that is the heart of this book. You may have a diagnosis, but you do not have to live a diagnosed identity.

The Awakening

This book is not about pretending mental health challenges don't exist. It's not about denying pain, trauma, or diagnosis. It's about reclaiming authorship. It's about learning to live beyond the labels that once controlled you. It's about discovering that the mind is trainable, just like the body, and that freedom is not found in perfection, but in practice.

It's about the moment the light turns on and everything that was once dark becomes visible, understandable, and transformable.

This is the story of how I awakened and how you can too.

WILLIAM "SCOTT" FAULKNER'S MEMORABILIA

THS number one
in football
Terriers have a right to be proud

2
The Elite Mindset™

"You're either elite or you're not."
— Kirby Smart[2]

Every athlete knows this truth:
TALENT gets you noticed.
DISCIPLINE keeps you in the game.
MINDSET determines who becomes **ELITE**.

For most of my life, I relied on talent. Speed. Strength. Instinct. Grit. Those things carried me through childhood, through high school, through the early years of football. But talent has a ceiling. Mindset does not.

When my life collapsed, when football died, when marriages fell apart, when the diagnosis hit, when the storms inside my mind were louder than anything outside; I didn't need more talent. I needed a new operating system. I needed what I now call, The Elite Mindset™.

And here's the truth most people never hear, The Elite Mindset™ is not about being better than others. It's about being better than the version of yourself that keeps you stuck. It's not superiority. It's not perfection. It's not ego. It's training. It's conditioning. It's reps. It's the same process an athlete uses to build strength, except now the weight is internal, and the gym is your mind.

The Mind Is a Muscle

If you've ever trained in a gym, you know this: *Muscles don't grow by accident*. They grow by resistance. The mind works the same way.

Every trigger, every emotional spike, every moment of anxiety, every depressive dip; these are not signs of weakness. They are resistance. They are the weight you lift mentally. And just like in the gym, the first reps feel impossible. Your legs shake. Your form collapses. Your breath shortens. Your body screams, "Stop!"

But if you keep showing up, something changes. The weight doesn't get lighter; you get stronger.

This is the foundation of The Elite Mindset™: You train your mind the same way you train your body with intentional reps, progressive overload, and a commitment to the process.

The Spirit Within Is Your Inner Coach

I'm not talking about religion. I'm not talking about doctrine. I'm not talking about church walls or denominational rules. I'm talking about the Spirit within you. The quiet, steady, unshakeable part of you that refuses to quit.

The part of you that whispers:

"You can do more than this."

"Get up."

"Try again."

"Stay on the trail."

Every athlete knows the difference between the external coach and the internal one. The external coach yells instructions. The internal coach whispers identity. And when you're fighting mental battles, when the diagnosis feels heavy, when the emotions feel unpredictable, when the storm clouds gather; the internal coach is the one that matters.

The Elite Mindset™ is built on this truth: There is a Spirit inside you that wants to be healed, wants to grow, and wants to rise; but it needs you to show up for the work.

The Trail

You'll hear me talk about "the trail" throughout this book. The trail is your path of growth. Your path of healing. Your path of becoming.

Some days the trail is clear. Some days it's muddy. Some days you lose it completely. But the trail is always there.

And The Elite Mindset™ is what keeps you on it. Not perfectly. Not flawlessly. Not without setbacks. But consistently. Because the trail doesn't require perfection. It requires returning.

The Elite Mindset™ Is Not a Cure

Let's get this straight: The Elite Mindset™ does not erase bipolar disorder. It does not eliminate anxiety. It does not magically remove depression. It does not replace medication. It does not make you immune to struggle.

This is not a miracle cure. This is not a spiritual bypass. This is not a motivational slogan. This is training. And training does not remove the weight. It builds the strength to carry it.

I still take medication. I still have days when the storm tries to pull me off the trail. I still have moments when the old patterns try to resurface.

But here's the difference: I no longer live as a slave to the diagnosis. I live as an athlete in training; aware, intentional, and equipped. The diagnosis is real. But the identity inside the diagnosis is optional.

The Three Pillars of The Elite Mindset™

Every athlete has fundamentals. Every team has a playbook. Every champion has a system. The Elite Mindset™ is built on three pillars:

1. **Awareness**
   You cannot change what you refuse to see. Awareness is the film room to

study your patterns, your triggers, your tendencies.

2. **Discipline**
   Not punishment. Not perfection. Discipline is simply doing the reps even when you don't feel like it.

3. **Identity**
   This is the game changer. Identity determines behavior. Behavior determines outcomes.

If you see yourself as broken, you will behave broken. If you see yourself as unstable, you will behave unstable. If you see yourself as powerless, you will behave powerless. But if you see yourself as someone in training, someone capable, someone growing, someone who can rise; your behavior will follow.

Identity is the engine. Mindset is the steering wheel. Your diagnosis is just the terrain.

The Elite Mindset™ Is a Choice Every Day

Some days you'll feel strong. Some days you'll feel weak. Some days you'll feel like you're sprinting. Some days you'll feel like you're crawling. But The Elite Mindset™ is not about how fast you move. It's about choosing to move at all.

It's about showing up. It's about staying on the trail. It's about listening to the Spirit within. It's about refusing to let the diagnosis write your story.

And here's the truth: You don't need to be perfect to be elite. You just need to be committed.

Where We Go From Here

In the next chapters, we're going to break down the actual tools, the mental training techniques that form The Elite Mindset™ system:

- ✓ Press Pause
- ✓ Identify Your Trigger

- ✓ Reframe Your Response
- ✓ Apply the Reframe in Real Time
- ✓ The Walkabout™
- ✓ Living Beyond Diagnosis

These are not theories. These are not slogans. These are not cute ideas. These are the tools that saved my life. And they can save yours.

3
Diagnosis Programming™

"The only thing that matters is what you do next."
— Bill Belichick[3]

Every athlete knows what it feels like to be labeled: "Too small." "Too slow." "Not coachable." "Raw talent." "High potential." "Head case." "Natural leader."

Labels are shortcuts. They're quick judgments. They're mental file folders people use to make sense of you.

But here's the danger: If you hear a label long enough, you start training like it's true. And once you train like it's true, you start living like it's true.

This is the heart of Diagnosis Programming™, the invisible process where a medical label becomes a mental identity, and a mental identity becomes a behavioral pattern. Most people don't even realize it's happening. But it happened to me. And if you're reading this, there's a good chance it's happening to you too.

The Day the Label Became the Identity

When I was diagnosed bipolar in 1993, the world didn't understand the condition. There were no podcasts. No social media. No mental health influencers. No trauma-informed therapists. No language for emotional regulation. There was only one message, "You're broken."

And I believed it.

I didn't just receive a diagnosis; I received an identity. I didn't hear, "You have bipolar disorder." I heard, "You ARE bipolar."

And that's the moment Diagnosis Programming™ began.

Because once you believe you are something, you unconsciously begin to behave like it. You start living into the label. You start fulfilling the prophecy. You start training for the wrong team.

It's like being handed the wrong playbook and running the wrong plays for years then wondering why the scoreboard looks the way it does.

The Power of a Story

Every diagnosis comes with a story attached to it.

For bipolar, the story was:

"Unstable." "Unpredictable."
"Dangerous." "Unreliable." "Unfixable."

For anxiety, the story might be:
"Fragile." "Nervous." "Overreactive."

For depression:
"Hopeless." "Lazy." "Unmotivated."

For ADHD:

"Scattered." "Disorganized." "Immature."

These stories are not written by the Spirit within you. They're written by society, by stigma, by misunderstanding, by fear.

But here's the truth: The story you attach to your diagnosis becomes the script you live out. And most people never question the script.

The Locker Room of the Mind

Imagine walking into a locker room where every locker has a nameplate. Except instead of your name, the plates say: "Bipolar." "Anxious." "Depressed." "Traumatized." "Addict." "Broken." "Damaged goods."

Now imagine being told, "Pick your locker. That's who you are now."

Most people don't pick consciously. They pick by default. They pick because they don't know they have a choice.

Diagnosis Programming™ is the process of putting your name on the wrong locker. And then spending years, sometimes decades, living out of it.

The Spirit Within You Knows Better

Here's where the spiritual grounding comes in. Not religion. Not doctrine. Not church politics. I'm talking about the Spirit within you. The part of you that knows truth even when your mind is confused.

The Spirit within you does not identify with brokenness. It does not identify with labels. It does not identify with limitations. The Spirit within you knows who you are beneath the diagnosis. It knows your strength. It knows your resilience. It knows your potential. It knows your identity.

And it whispers, "This is not who you are. This is something you experience not something you become."

Diagnosis Programming™ happens when the mind stops listening to the Spirit and starts listening to the label. The Elite Mindset™ is the process of reversing that.

The Playbook Problem

Every diagnosis comes with a playbook, a set of expectations, behaviors, and assumptions.

For bipolar, the playbook says, "You will be unstable." "You will be impulsive." "You will be unpredictable." "You will ruin relationships." "You will sabotage your life."

For years, I ran that playbook. Not because I wanted to. Not because I chose to. But because I didn't know there was another one.

Here's the truth: Your diagnosis may explain your tendencies, but it does not dictate your identity. You can have a diagnosis without running the diagnosis playbook. You can have symptoms without surrendering your story. You can have struggles without losing your identity.

The Mental Weight You Don't Realize You're Carrying

Diagnosis Programming™ is heavy. It's like carrying a weighted vest you didn't know you put on. Every decision feels harder. Every emotion feels heavier. Every setback feels personal. Every mistake feels like proof. *And the worst part?* You start expecting yourself to fail. You start assuming you'll lose control. You start believing you're incapable. You start predicting your own downfall.

This is not the diagnosis talking. This is the programming talking. And programming can be rewritten.

The Turning Point: Awareness

The first step to break Diagnosis Programming™ is awareness. You cannot change what you cannot see. You must become aware of:

- The story you've attached to your diagnosis
- The identity you've built around it
- The behaviors you've justified because of it
- The limitations you've accepted without questioning
- The patterns you've repeated because you believed you had no choice

Awareness is the film room. It's where you study the plays you've been running. It's where you see the patterns clearly for the first time. And once you see it, you can't unsee it.

The Spirit + The Mind + The Identity

Breaking Diagnosis Programming™ requires three things:

1. **The Spirit:** Your inner grounding. Your truth. Your compass. Your identity beneath the noise.
2. **The Mind:** Your thoughts. Your patterns. Your triggers. Your interpretations.
3. **The Identity:** The story you choose to live from. The locker you choose to claim. The playbook you choose to run.

When these three align, you become unstoppable. When they're misaligned, you feel lost. Diagnosis Programming™ is misalignment. The Elite Mindset™ is alignment.

The Good News

Diagnosis Programming™ is powerful, but it is not permanent. It can be rewritten. It can be replaced. It can be dismantled. It can be healed.

And the next chapters will show you exactly how.

4
Press Pause

"You can't go out and practice average
and then expect to play great."
— Tom Brady[4]

Every athlete knows the importance of the first rep. It's the rep that sets the tone. The rep that wakes up the nervous system. The rep that tells the body, "We're doing this."

In mental training, the first rep is *Press Pause.*

It sounds simple. It sounds small. It sounds almost too basic to matter. But Press Pause is the difference between reacting from old programming and responding from a new identity. It is the difference between losing control and taking control. Between spiraling and stabilizing. Between living from the diagnosis and living beyond it.

Press Pause is the moment you interrupt the automatic pattern. The moment you step out of the storm long enough to see what's *actually* happening. It is the first rep of The Elite Mindset™.

The Moment Before the Moment

Every emotional reaction has two parts:

1. The trigger
2. The response

Most people think the response is the problem. It's not. The real problem is the speed between the trigger and the response.

For people living with mental health struggles, especially bipolar, anxiety, trauma, or ADHD, that speed is lightning fast. Instant. Automatic. Unconscious. It feels like there's no space between what happens and what you do next.

Press Pause creates that space. It slows the moment down. It interrupts autopilot. It gives you a window, even if it's only two seconds, to choose differently.

In sports, this is called game speed awareness. The great athletes don't play faster, they see faster. The game slows down for them. Press Pause slows down the game of your mind.

The Physiology of the Pause

This isn't magic. It's not mystical. It's not, "Just breathe and everything will be fine." Press Pause works because of neurology.

When you're triggered, your brain shifts into survival mode. Fight. Flight. Freeze. Fawn. Your prefrontal cortex, the part responsible for logic, reasoning, and decision-making, goes offline.

Press Pause brings it back online. It's the mental equivalent of calling a timeout when the defense is collapsing on you. You step back. You breathe. You reset the play. The body calms. The mind clears. The Spirit speaks. And suddenly, you're not reacting. You're choosing.

The Spiritual Grounding of the Pause

Press Pause is not just a mental technique. It's a spiritual one. When you pause, you reconnect with the Spirit within you. The part of you that is steady, grounded, and unshaken by the chaos of the moment.

The pause is where the Spirit whispers:

"You are not your reaction."

"You are not your diagnosis."

"You are not the storm."

"Stay on the trail."

The pause is where you remember who you are. It's where identity overrides impulse. Where truth overrides fear. Where grounding overrides chaos. Press Pause is the doorway back to yourself.

The Athletic Analogy: The Reset Between Plays

Football taught me something I didn't understand until years later: Between every play, there is a reset. The whistle blows. The players stand up. They jog back to the huddle. They breathe. They reset the formation. They call the next play.

No matter how good or bad the last play was, there is always a reset. Press Pause is your reset between plays.

What Press Pause Is NOT

Press Pause is *NOT*:

- Avoidance
- Suppression
- Denial

- Pretending you're fine
- Ignoring your emotions
- "Just calming down"

Press Pause *IS*:

- Awareness
- Grounding
- Interrupting autopilot
- Creating space
- Choosing your next move

It is not weakness. It is not passivity. It is not surrender. It is strength. It is discipline. It is training.

How to Press Pause

Here is the practical, simple, repeatable process:

1. **Notice the spike**. The moment your heart rate jumps, your chest tightens, your

thoughts speed up, or your emotions surge. That's your cue.

2. **Stop the forward momentum.** You don't walk away. You don't explode. You don't react. You simply pause.

3. **Take one slow breath.** Not five. Not ten. Just one. Inhale through the nose. Exhale through the mouth. This signals your nervous system to shift out of survival mode.

4. **Anchor yourself.** Silently say something like, "I'm here." "I'm safe." "I'm choosing." "Stay on the trail."

5. **Let the moment slow down.** You don't force clarity. You allow it. And in that space, even if it's only a second, you regain control.

Why This Works for Mental Health

People with mental health struggles often feel like their emotions hijack them. Press Pause gives you the steering wheel back.

It doesn't eliminate emotion. It doesn't erase the trigger. It doesn't cure the diagnosis. But it gives you something far more powerful: *Choice.*

Choice is the foundation of freedom. Choice is the beginning of healing. Choice is the first step beyond the diagnosis. Press Pause is the tool that makes choice possible.

The First Rep Is the Hardest

Just like in the gym, the first rep is always the hardest. Your mind will resist. Your emotions will push back. Your old programming will try to take over.

But every time you Press Pause, you strengthen the neural pathway. You reinforce the identity of someone who chooses to respond rather than react. You build the muscle of mental control. And over time, the pause becomes natural. Automatic. Instinctive.

Press Pause Is the Foundation

Every tool that comes next: Identify Your Trigger, Reframe Your Response, Apply the Reframe, The Walkabout™, Living Beyond Diagnosis, all depend on this one skill.

Press Pause is the foundation. The anchor. The first rep. The reset. The doorway. Without it, the rest of the system collapses. With it, everything becomes possible.

5
Identify Your Trigger

"Awareness is the first step to improvement."
— Nick Saban[5]

Every athlete knows that the game is not won on the field, it's won in the film room. You study tendencies. You study patterns. You study what the opponent does before they do it.

Mental health works the same way.

Your emotions, your reactions, your impulses, they all have patterns. They all have tells. They all have precursors. But most people never learn to see them.

They only notice the explosion, not the fuse. They only notice the reaction, not the spark.

They only notice the storm, not the shift in the wind.

Identifying your *trigger* is learning to read the weather of your mind. It's learning to see the clouds forming before the lightning strikes. It's learning to recognize the early signs, the subtle cues, that tell you a reaction is coming.

This is not about fear. This is not about hypervigilance. This is not about walking on eggshells around your own emotions. This is about awareness which is the second pillar of The Elite Mindset™.

Triggers Are Not the Enemy

Most people treat triggers like landmines. They fear them. Avoid them. Deny them. Hide from them.

But triggers are not the enemy. Triggers are information. They are signals. Indicators. Clues. Data points.

They tell you where the wound is. They tell you where the pattern lives. They tell you where the work needs to be done.

A trigger is not a sign of weakness. It's a sign of where strength is being built. In the gym, the muscle that shakes is the muscle that's growing. In mental training, the trigger that activates is the trigger that's healing.

The Three Types of Triggers

Not all triggers are the same. And if you don't know which type you're dealing with, you'll misinterpret the moment.

1. **Internal Triggers**: These come from inside you.

   Examples: A sudden shift in mood, a spike in energy, a drop in motivation, a racing thought, a memory, a physical sensation.

Internal triggers are the hardest to spot because they feel like "you". But they're not you. They're signals.

2. **External Triggers:** These come from outside you.

   Examples: A tone of voice, a facial expression, a stressful environment, a loud noise, a conflict, a demand, a disappointment.

   External triggers are easier to identify, but harder to control.

3. **Identity Triggers:** These are the deepest ones, tied to your story, your past, your wounds, and your beliefs.

   Examples: Feeling misunderstood, disrespected, abandoned, powerless, judged, or unseen.

   Identity triggers hit the hardest because they activate old programming. They are the triggers that pull you back into the diagnosis identity if you're not careful.

The Athletic Analogy: Reading the Defense

In football, a great quarterback doesn't just run the play. He reads the defense. He sees the safety creeping up. He notices the linebacker shifting weight. He recognizes the cornerback's eyes. He senses the blitz before it happens. He doesn't panic. He doesn't freeze. He adjusts.

Identifying your trigger is reading the defense of your mind.

The Spirit's Role in Trigger Awareness

The Spirit within you is not loud. It doesn't shout. It doesn't panic. It doesn't rush. It whispers. It nudges. It alerts. It signals.

When you learn to listen, the Spirit will often warn you before your emotions do. A tightening in the chest. A heaviness in the stomach. A shift in your breathing. A quiet sense of "something's off".

This is *discernment*. The Spirit is your internal weather radar, always scanning, always sensing, always guiding.

The Trigger Map

Every person has a unique pattern of triggers, a personal "Trigger Map." Once you map them, you gain clarity. You begin to see:

- What sets you off
- What drains you
- What overwhelms you
- What destabilizes you
- What awakens old wounds
- What activates old identities

A Trigger Map is not a list of weaknesses. It's a list of opportunities. Every trigger is a doorway to growth.

The Power of Naming

There is power in naming a trigger. When you name something, you take authority over it.

You shift from:
"I don't know what's happening,"
to "I know exactly what this is."

You shift from:
"I'm losing control,"
to "I'm recognizing a pattern."

You shift from:
"This is who I am,"
to "This is something I'm experiencing."

Naming a trigger is the moment you reclaim authorship.

Awareness is the first rep. Repetition builds strength. Strength builds stability. You are training your mind. You are building your identity. You are staying on the trail.

CALL TO ACTION

YOUR TRIGGER REPS

1. **Identify One Internal Trigger:** Something inside you that shifts your emotional state.
2. **Identify One External Trigger:** Something outside you that consistently affects your mood or reactions.
3. **Identify One Identity Trigger:** Something that hits your story, your wounds, or your sense of self.
4. **Write Them Down:** Not in your head. On paper. In your phone. In a notebook. Somewhere real.
5. **Notice Them This Week:** Not to avoid them, but to recognize them.

6
Reframe Your Response

"I can't control what happens around me.
I can only control how I respond."
—Tom Brady[6]

If *Press Pause* is the first rep and *Identifying Your Trigger* is reading the defense, then *Reframing Your Response* is calling an audible at the line of scrimmage.

It's the moment you look at the situation, recognize the pattern, and say: "Nope. Not running that play again."

Reframing is not pretending. It's not sugar-coating. It's not lying to yourself. It's not "positive vibes only".

(If positive vibes cured mental health, health food stores would hospitals.)

Reframing is the skill of changing the meaning of the moment so you can change your response to it. It's the mental equivalent of shifting your weight, adjusting your stance, and hitting the same weight with better form. Same weight. Better technique. Different outcome.

Why Reframing Matters

Your brain is a meaning-making machine. It doesn't just experience things, it interprets them. And the interpretation becomes the emotion. The emotion becomes the reaction. The reaction becomes the pattern. The pattern becomes the identity.

Reframing interrupts that chain. It's the moment you say: "I'm not letting my old story decide how I respond to this moment."

Reframing is not about changing reality. It's about changing your relationship to it.

The Athletic Analogy: Film Room Reframes

Every athlete has watched film of themselves doing something stupid. A blown coverage. A missed tackle. A lazy rep. A moment where you think, *Why did I do THAT?*

But film room isn't about shame. It's about reframing. You watch the mistake. You understand the mistake. You learn from the mistake. You adjust the next rep.

Reframing your response is the film room of your mind except you're doing it in real time.

The Spirit's Role in Reframing

The Spirit within you is not interested in your old story. It's not invested in your diagnosis identity. It's not attached to your past patterns. The Spirit is always pointing you toward truth.

When you reframe, you are aligning your mind with the Spirit's perspective. You're saying: “I’m not reacting from fear. I’m responding from truth.”

What Reframing Is NOT

Reframing is NOT:

- “Everything is fine.” (It’s not. You’re sweating through your shirt.)
- “This doesn’t bother me.” (It does. Your eye is twitching.)
- “I’m totally calm.” (You’re absolutely not.)
- “I love conflict.” (No, you don’t. You’re human.)
- “This is great!” (It’s not great. It’s a dumpster fire.)

Reframing is not delusion. It’s direction.

The Three Types of Reframes

1. **The Perspective Reframe:**
   Shifts how you see the situation.

   Example: Instead of, "They're disrespecting me," shift to, "They're overwhelmed and projecting."

2. **The Identity Reframe:**
   Shifts how you see yourself in the moment.

   Example: Instead of, "I'm losing control," shift to, "I'm recognizing a pattern and choosing differently." These are the most powerful because they break Diagnosis Programming™.

3. **The Opportunity Reframe:**
   Shifts what the moment means for your growth.

   Example: Instead of, "This trigger is ruining my day," shift to, "This trigger is showing me where I'm getting stronger."

The Formula:
Trigger → Meaning → Emotion → Response

Here's the chain most people never see:

Trigger → Meaning → Emotion → Response

Most people think the trigger causes the emotion. It doesn't. The meaning you attach to the trigger causes the emotion. Reframing changes the meaning. And when you change the meaning, you change the emotion. When you change the emotion, you change the response. When you change the response, you change the pattern. When you change the pattern, you change your identity.

This is how you live beyond the diagnosis. Not by force. Not by denial. Not by pretending. By reframing.

The Humor Reassurance

Sometimes the best assurance can be found in humor. Not sarcasm. Not self-mockery.

Not avoidance. Just a simple, grounded, human moment of: "Wow! My brain really tried *it* today."

Humor breaks tension. Humor interrupts spirals. Humor resets the nervous system. A well-timed laugh is sometimes the most spiritual thing you can do.

How to Reframe in Real Time

1. Press Pause: Creates the space.
2. Identify the Trigger: Gives you clarity.
3. Ask one question: "What else could this mean?"
4. Choose the most helpful meaning.
5. Respond from the new meaning.

You're training your mind. You're building new patterns. You're staying on the trail.

CALL TO ACTION

YOUR REFRAME REPS

1. Pick one trigger from Chapter Five. Just one.
2. Write down the meaning you normally attach to it. Be honest. No judgment.
3. Write down one alternative meaning. Not perfect. Just possible.
4. Practice choosing the new meaning once this week. Just once. One rep.
5. Celebrate the rep. Even if it was messy. Even if it was only 10% successful.

7
Apply the Reframe in the Moment

"Pressure is a privilege."
— Patrick Mahomes[7]

Reframing in theory is easy. Reframing in the moment is a whole different ballgame.

It's like practicing free throws in an empty gym versus shooting them in the fourth quarter with the game on the line, the crowd screaming, and your legs shaking like you just did leg day after skipping it for six months straight.

Anyone can be at peace when nothing is happening. Anyone can be calm when life is quiet. Anyone can be wise when no one is pushing their buttons.

But applying the reframe in the moment, when the trigger hits, when the emotion spikes, when the old identity tries to take the wheel, that's where the real training begins.

This chapter is about execution. Not perfection. Execution.

The Gap Between Knowing and Doing

Every athlete knows this truth: There is a massive difference between knowing the playbook and running the play. You can memorize every formation. You can study every route. You can quote every coaching point. But when the ball is snapped, instinct takes over. And instinct is built through reps not knowledge.

Applying the reframe in the moment is the mental equivalent of running the play under pressure. It's not about being flawless. It's about being present. It's about choosing the new meaning even when the old meaning is screaming for attention.

The Emotional Blitz

Triggers don't show up politely. They don't knock on the door and ask if it's a good time. They blitz. They hit fast. They hit hard. They hit without warning.

Your heart rate spikes. Your breathing changes. Your thoughts speed up. Your body tenses. Your mind shifts into survival mode.

This is the moment where most people lose control. Not because they're weak, but because they've never been trained. The emotional blitz is not the problem. The lack of preparation is.

The Spirit's Whisper in the Chaos

When the emotional blitz hits, the Spirit within you does not panic. It whispers:

"Pause."

"Breathe."

"You've been here before."

"Choose the new meaning."

"Stay on the trail."

The Spirit is the calm in the chaos. The anchor in the storm. The coach in the headset saying, "You know what to do. Run the play."

The Humor Advantage

Sometimes the best way to break the emotional blitz is to laugh at how dramatic your brain can be. Your brain will say things like: "This is the end." "Everything is ruined." "We should move to a cabin in the woods and never speak to anyone again."

And sometimes the most elite response is: "Okay brain… relax. We're not being chased by a bear." Humor is a legitimate mental health tool. Use it.

The Four-Second Window

Here's the secret most people never learn: You have about four seconds between the trigger and the reaction. Those four seconds are your opportunity.

Press Pause creates the space. Identifying the trigger gives clarity. Reframing gives direction. But applying the reframe in the moment is what you do with those four seconds.

It's the difference between reacting and responding. Between repeating and rewriting. Between spiraling and stabilizing. Four seconds. That's all you need.

The Technique:
The 4-Step In-Moment Reframe

1. **Pause the impulse**: You don't move. You don't speak. You don't react. You freeze the autopilot.

2. **Name the trigger**: Not out loud. Just internally. “Identity trigger.” “Tone trigger.” “Abandonment trigger.” “Overwhelm trigger.” Naming it gives you authority.

3. **Choose the new meaning:** Ask, “What’s the most helpful meaning right now?” Not the prettiest. Not the most spiritual. The most helpful.

4. **Act from the new meaning**: This is the execution. This is the rep. This is The Elite Mindset™ in motion. Even if it’s messy. Even if it’s shaky. Even if it’s only 60% successful. It counts.

The Athletic Analogy: Muscle Memory

When you first learn a new movement, it feels awkward. Your form is off. Your timing is off. But with reps, something changes. Your body learns. Your nervous system adapts. Your muscles remember.

Applying the reframe in the moment works the same way. At first, it feels clunky. Forced. Unnatural. But with reps, it becomes instinct. You stop reacting from the diagnosis. You start responding from identity.

The Truth: You Won't Nail It Every Time

You're going to mess this up sometimes. You'll forget to pause. You'll miss the trigger. You'll choose the wrong meaning. That's okay. This is training, not perfection.

Every athlete has *off* days. But they keep showing up. And so will you.

You're training your mind. You're building new patterns. You're strengthening your identity. You're staying on the trail.

CALL TO ACTION

YOUR IN-MOMENT REFRAME REPS

1. Pick one trigger from your Trigger Map. Just one.
2. Commit to catching it ONE time this week.
3. Use the 4-Step In-Moment Reframe: Pause. Name. Choose. Act.
4. Afterward, write down what happened, not to judge yourself, but to learn from yourself.
5. Celebrate the rep. Even if it was imperfect. Even if it was only a partial win.

8
The Walkabout™

"It's not the will to win.
It's the will to prepare to win."
— Bear Bryant[8]

Every great coach has a signature move. A technique. A philosophy. A tool that separates them from the rest.

For you it's The Walkabout™.

This isn't just a cute name. It's not a gimmick. It's not a trendy mental health hack. The Walkabout™ is a game changer, a method that rewires your self-talk, resets your emotional state, and reconnects you to the Spirit within you.

What Is a Walkabout™?

A Walkabout™ is a guided internal conversation. It is a mental journey you take with yourself when you feel overwhelmed, triggered, confused, or emotionally flooded.

It's not walking away. It's not shutting down. It's not avoiding the moment. It's stepping into the moment with clarity, compassion, and control.

A Walkabout™ is:

- A reset
- A grounding technique
- A mental timeout
- A spiritual check-in
- A conversation with your wiser self
- A way to shift your emotional state without losing your identity

It's the mental equivalent of stepping off the field, taking a knee, and letting the coach talk you through the next play. Except the coach is you.

Why The Walkabout™ Works

Because it interrupts the emotional autopilot. When you're triggered, your brain wants to sprint into old patterns:

- "Here we go again."
- "I can't handle this."
- "This always happens."
- "I'm losing control."
- "This is who I am."

The Walkabout™ stops that sprint. It slows the moment down. It shifts your internal dialogue. It gives you space to breathe, to think, to choose.

It's the bridge between the trigger and the new identity. The moment when you stop reacting from the diagnosis and start responding from The Elite Mindset™.

The Athletic Analogy: The Sideline Reset

Every athlete knows the power of the sideline. You come off the field after a bad play and the coach grabs your facemask (gently… hopefully) and says, "Look at me. Slow down. Here's what happened. Here's what we're going to do next."

The Walkabout™ is your sideline reset except you don't need a coach, a whistle, or a stadium. You carry the sideline within you.

The Spiritual Grounding of The Walkabout™

The Walkabout™ is not just mental. It's spiritual. It's the moment where you reconnect with the Spirit within you. The Spirit doesn't shame you. It doesn't rush you. It doesn't condemn you. It guides you.

It reminds you, "You are not the storm. You are not the diagnosis. You are not the reaction. You are the one choosing the next step."

The Walkabout™ is how you hear that voice.

The Humor Factor

Sometimes your brain acts like a toddler who missed nap time and ate an entire bag of sugary candy. It throws tantrums. It catastrophizes everything. It says things like: "We're doomed." "Let's move to the mountains and raise goats."

A Walkabout™ lets you respond with: "Okay, buddy… let's take a little walk and calm down." Humor reminds you that your brain is dramatic, not dangerous.

The Walkabout™ Method: Step by Step

1. **Step Out of the Immediate Emotion** Say to yourself: "Alright, let's take a Walkabout™." This signals your brain to shift from reaction to reflection.

2. **Ask: "What am I actually feeling right now?"**

   Angry? Hurt? Overwhelmed? Embarrassed? Afraid? Triggered? Tired? Hungry? (Yes, hunger counts. Half of my worst decisions were made on an empty stomach.)

3. **Ask: "Where is this coming from?"**

   Identify the trigger. Internal? External? Identity-based? You're not judging; you're locating.

4. **Ask: "What story am I telling myself?"**

   "This person doesn't respect me." "I'm failing." "I'm not enough." "This always happens." This is where the old programming shows up.

5. **Ask: "Is that story actually true?"**

   Most of the time, the answer is: "No, not really."

6. **Ask: "What's a more helpful story right now?"**

   "This is a trigger, not a truth." "I'm overwhelmed, not broken." "I can choose my response." "I'm staying on the trail."

7. **Choose your next step.**

   Not ten steps. Not the whole plan. Just the next step. Breathe. Walk away. Speak calmly. Say nothing. Ask for clarity. Take a break. Drink water. Reset.

The Walkabout™ ends with action; not rumination.

Why The Walkabout™ Is a Game Changer

Because it changes the conversation in your mind. Most people talk to themselves like an enemy. The Walkabout™ teaches you to talk to yourself like a coach. Most people react from old wounds. The Walkabout™ helps you respond from new identity. Most people spiral. The Walkabout™ stabilizes. This method is not just a tool; it's a transformation.

CALL TO ACTION

YOUR WALKABOUT™ REPS

1. Choose one moment this week to practice a Walkabout™. Not a crisis. Not a meltdown. Just a moment of tension.
2. Walk through the seven steps. Even if it feels awkward. Even if it feels forced.
3. Write down what you discovered. What emotion was underneath? What story were you telling yourself? What new story did you choose?
4. Celebrate the rep. This is you taking control of your mind. This is you rewriting your identity. This is you staying on the trail.

9
Living Beyond Diagnosis

"If you don't believe in yourself,
why should anyone else?"
— Tom Brady[9]

There comes a moment in every athlete's journey when the game slows down. Not because the game changed but because they changed. Their awareness sharpened. Their instincts refined. Their confidence deepened. Their identity solidified.

Thc samc thing happcns in mental health. There comes a moment when you realize: "My diagnosis is real but it no longer defines me."

This is the moment you begin living beyond the diagnosis. Not in denial. Not in delusion.

Not in rebellion. Not in shame. But in freedom. Freedom that is earned. Freedom that is trained. Freedom that is built rep by rep, moment by moment, choice by choice.

The Diagnosis Is Real:
But It's Not the Whole Story

Living beyond the diagnosis does NOT mean:

- You're cured
- You're symptom-free
- You never struggle
- You never wobble
- You never need medication

Living beyond the diagnosis means: You no longer build your identity around the diagnosis. You no longer wake up expecting chaos. You no longer let the label write your story.

You live *with* the diagnosis, but you don't live *as* the diagnosis. That distinction changes everything.

The Athletic Analogy: Playing With an Injury

Every athlete eventually plays with something: a strained hamstring, a sore shoulder, a bruised rib. They don't pretend the injury isn't there. They don't shame themselves for it. They manage it. They adapt. They train around it. They stay in the game.

Mental health is the same. You don't pretend the diagnosis isn't there. You don't shame yourself for it. You manage it. You adapt. You train around it. You stay in the game. This is living beyond the diagnosis.

The Spirit Within You Wants to Heal

There is a Spirit inside you; steady, grounded, and wise, that wants healing more than you do. It wants peace. It wants clarity.

It wants stability. It wants freedom. It wants wholeness.

The Spirit is not intimidated by your diagnosis. It's not discouraged by your past. It sees the truth of who you are *not* the version you became in survival mode.

Living beyond the diagnosis is aligning your daily life with that truth. It's letting the Spirit lead instead of the symptoms.

The Identity Shift

Living beyond the diagnosis requires one fundamental shift: You stop asking, "What's wrong with me?" and start asking, "What's possible for me?"

This shift changes your posture, your decisions, your habits, your relationships, your self-talk, and ultimately your future.

Identity drives behavior. Behavior drives outcomes. Outcomes reinforce identity.

Living beyond the diagnosis breaks the old cycle and builds a new one.

Operating The Elite Mindset™

By this point, you've learned the tools:

- Press Pause
- Identify Your Trigger
- Reframe Your Response
- Apply the Reframe
- The Walkabout™

These tools form a new operating system. The Elite Mindset™ does three things:

1. **Stabilizes your emotions,** not by suppressing them, but by understanding them.
2. **Strengthens your identity**, not by pretending, but by choosing.
3. **Rewires your patterns,** not overnight, but through reps.

The Humor of Healing

Healing is messy. Some days you'll feel like a monk. Some days you'll feel like a raccoon in a dumpster. Some days you'll feel like a motivational speaker. Some days you'll feel like you need a nap, a snack, and a therapist, in that order.

That's okay. Humor keeps you human. Living beyond the diagnosis means you can laugh again; not because everything is perfect, but because you're no longer drowning.

The Trail Ahead

Living beyond the diagnosis is not a destination; it's a trail. Some days the trail is smooth. Some days it's rocky. Some days it's uphill. Some days you lose it. Some days you find it again.

But the trail is always there. And as long as you keep walking; even slowly, even limping, even crawling; you are living beyond the diagnosis.

Hope lives on the trail. Healing lives on the trail. Identity lives on the trail. Freedom lives on the trail. And the Spirit walks it with you.

You are living beyond the diagnosis. You are building a new identity. You are staying on the trail. And hope lives here.

CALL TO ACTION

YOUR BEYOND THE DIAGNOSIS REPS

1. Write a new identity statement. Not who you *were,* instead, *who* you are becoming. Example: “I am someone who chooses my responses.” “I am someone who grows through challenges.” “I am someone who stays on the trail.”
2. Choose one daily habit that supports your new identity. Small. Simple. Repeatable.
3. Notice one moment this week where you lived beyond the diagnosis. It might be tiny. It might be subtle. But it counts.
4. Celebrate it. Not because it was perfect but because it was progress.

10
The Call Forward

"You run through the smoke.
You don't run from it."
—Mike Alstott[10]

There comes a moment in every comeback story when the crowd goes quiet, the field lights burn bright, and the athlete realizes, *I'm not who I used to be*. Not the broken version. Not the diagnosed version. Not the defeated version.

A new identity has emerged. One built through reps, resilience, and relentless truth.

This is that moment for you.

This is the moment when you stop looking back at the wreckage and start looking forward at the road. This is the moment where you stop asking, “Can I do this?” and start declaring, “I was built for this.”

This is the call forward.

You Are Not Who You Were

You’ve walked through the fire. You’ve faced the storm. You’ve confronted the diagnosis. You’ve challenged the old identity. You’ve trained your mind. You’ve learned the tools. You’ve stayed on the trail.

You are not who you were when this book began. You are not the person who felt powerless. You are not the person who reacted without thinking. You are not the person who believed the diagnosis was destiny.

You are someone new. Someone stronger. Someone wiser. Someone grounded. Someone intentional. Someone capable. Someone awake. This is the victory.

Winning Doesn't Mean the Game Is Easy

You will still have triggers. You will still have emotions. You will still have tough days. You will still have moments where the old identity tries to sneak back in like an uninvited guest who "just happened to be in the neighborhood."

But here's the difference: You now have a playbook. A system. Tools. Awareness. Identity. Spirit. Strength.

Winning doesn't mean the game is easy. Winning means you know how to play it.

The Spirit Within You Is Not Done

The Spirit that carried you through this book is not done with you. It's not finished. It's not tired. It's not discouraged. It's ready. Ready to guide you. Ready to strengthen you. Ready to lead you into the next chapter of your life.

The Spirit within you is undefeated. And now you're learning to live from that place.

The Humor of Victory

Let's keep it real, winning doesn't mean you become a flawless, enlightened guru who floats through life like you're sponsored by essential oils. You're still human. You'll still lose your keys. You'll still get irritated at slow drivers. You'll still have days where your brain says, "Let's panic for no reason." That's okay.

Victory isn't about perfection. It's about direction. It's about choosing the trail again and again. It's about laughing at yourself when you need to.

Your Life Is Not a Recovery Story, It's a Redemption Story

Recovery is about getting back what was lost. Redemption is about becoming something greater than you imagined.

You didn't just recover from the diagnosis. You redeemed it. You turned pain into wisdom. You turned struggle into strength. You turned chaos into clarity. You turned survival into purpose.

Your life is not a recovery story. It's a redemption story. And redemption stories are the ones that save lives.

The Call Forward

This is the moment when you step into the life you were created to live. Not the life shaped by fear. Not the life shaped by diagnosis. Not the life shaped by old programming.

The life shaped by: identity, truth, Spirit, discipline, resilience, purpose, and freedom. The life shaped by The Elite Mindset™. The life shaped by the trail you now know how to walk.

Live boldly. Live intentionally. Live awake. Live grounded. Live beyond the diagnosis.

Live as the person you were always meant to be.

The world needs that version of you. Your family needs that version of you. Your future needs that version of you. And you deserve that version of you.

The Trail Doesn't End Here

This book ends. Your journey does not.

You will keep growing. You will keep learning. You will keep strengthening. You will keep choosing. You will keep rising.

And when you stumble, because you will, you now know how to get back on the trail. You know how to: Press Pause, Identify the Trigger, Reframe the Response, Apply the Reframe, Take a Walkabout™, Live Beyond the Diagnosis.

You have everything you need.

CALL TO ACTION

YOUR FINAL REPS

1. Write your "Call Forward Statement." One sentence. One declaration. One truth.

   Example: "I am living beyond my diagnosis and stepping into the life I was created for."

2. Choose one habit you will carry forward from this book. Just one. Make it yours.

3. Share your journey with someone. Not to impress them, but to inspire them.

4. Stay on the trail. Always.

Bonus Story
The Trail to Becoming

"You can go your own way."
— Fleetwood Mac[11]

There was a time when I believed the goal was to reach the end of the trail. I thought somewhere ahead there was a clearing, a final place where everything would make sense. A place where I would finally feel complete, finished, and whole. If I could just keep moving, just endure a little longer, I would arrive.

But the trail kept going. It bent around corners I did not expect. The elevation increased when I was tired. It disappeared into the fog when I was looking for clarity.

And just when I thought I was close to the end, the trail would open into something new. Another stretch, another path, sometimes a fork in the path and a choice to be made, another invitation.

For a long time, that frustrated me because I was chasing an ending.

Then one day something shifted. Not on the trail but inside of me.

I stopped asking, "How much further?" And started asking, "What is here, right here, right now?"

And that is when I began to see it:

The trail was never something to finish. It was something to live, to experience, to learn from, to be transformed by.

On the trail I found surprises I would have missed had I been in a rush. Moments of beauty tucked between the bends. Clarity that only came after moving through fog and confusion. Strength that only appeared after I thought I had none left.

On the trail I was being changed. Not at the end. Not at some imagined destination. But right there. In the middle of the trail. In the middle of moving and pausing along the trail.

The First Principle of Becoming,
You Are Never Finished

There is no final version of you waiting at the end of the trail. There is only you *becoming*.

And the trail… it never ends. But that is not a curse. It is a gift.

Because if the trail never ends, then neither does growth. Neither does discovery. Neither does the unfolding of who you were meant to be.

So now, I don't look for the end anymore. I don't measure my life by how close I am to being done.

Instead, I align myself with something deeper. I accept that I am always on the trail. And in that acceptance, something unexpected happens.

I feel lighter; not burdened by an ending. I feel freer; not driven to finish. I feel more alive; not *done*. Because the trail is no longer something I am straining to get through.

It is a place where I choose to stay in growth mode. Not as something to endure, but something to embrace.

The Second Principle of Becoming, You Are Never Broken

For a long time, I thought that if something wasn't working for me, it meant something was broken. That I was broken. That somewhere along the trail, I had been damaged in a way that needed fixing before I could move forward again.

But then I remembered a lesson from when I was a kid.

I told my dad I couldn't cut the grass because the lawn mower was broken. It wouldn't start. I had pulled the cord again and again and nothing happened. So, in my mind, the conclusion was simple: the mower was broken.

My dad didn't argue. He simply said, "Oh, you can't mow because the lawn mower is broken? Let's go take a look."

We walked to the mower. He asked me to pull the cord. I did. Once, twice, three times. Nothing.

Then he went to the garage, grabbed a screw-driver, removed one screw, and took off what I later learned was the air filter. He held it up and asked what I noticed.

"It's really dirty," I said.

Then he asked a question I have never forgotten, “If I put this in front of your mouth, could you breathe?”

“No.”

“Neither can a lawn mower.”

He cleaned the filter until it looked new, put it back, tightened the single screw, and told me to pull the cord again.

Once. Twice. It started right up.

It wasn’t broken after all.

“You thought it was broken,” he said. “The truth is it was giving you signals all along. You just didn’t know how to read them.”

That lesson didn’t just apply to lawnmowers. It applied directly to my life. And it applies to yours as well.

We are not broken. We are responding.

What we often label as *broken* in ourselves is usually something else:

- A signal we've been ignoring
- A rhythm we've drifted away from
- A small habit we've neglected
- A part of us that cannot breathe under the weight it's carrying

Just like that engine, we are designed to function, to move, to grow. But even good systems require attention.

On the trail there will be moments when you feel stuck. Moments when you don't "start" like you used to. Moments when things feel harder than they should.

And you assume something is fundamentally wrong.

But what if that's not the truth at all? What if you are not broken? What if you are being signaled?

The trail teaches us that there is a difference between being broken and being misaligned. Between being broken and needing tending to.

Sometimes all it takes is cleaning the filter. A small adjustment. A return to something simple. A moment of awareness.

And suddenly you can breathe again. You can move again. You can continue on the trail.

Because here's what happens, if we believe we are broken, we stop. We step off the trail. We wait for someone to fix us. We do nothing.

But if we understand that we are *not* broken; we may stop, but we never leave the trail. We listen. We adjust. We respond.

Because just like the trail never ends, the process of tending to ourselves never ends either.

And that is not a burden. It is an invitation.

You are not a broken machine. You are a living, breathing person learning to notice what you need in order to keep going.

And sometimes the difference between being stuck and moving forward is as simple and powerful as cleaning the filter.

The Third Principle of Becoming, Honesty and Patience with Yourself

If the trail never ends, and you are not broken along the way, then how you treat yourself on the trail matters more than anything.

Becoming isn't just about movement. It is about how you respond when things don't go as planned.

There are moments on the trail when you miss the turn. You thought you were going the right way. You were confident. You were moving forward.

Then suddenly, "Oh no, I'm off the trail."

And in those moments, something interesting happens. Most of us do *not* respond with grace. Instead, we respond with judgment, "What are you doing?" "How did you miss the signs?" "You should know better by now."

We speak to ourselves in ways we would never speak to someone walking beside us.

But think about this, when you're using a navigation system and you miss a turn, it doesn't say, "Hey you idiot, you missed your turn again."

No.

It doesn't shame you. It doesn't panic. It doesn't insult you.

It simply says, "Recalculating."

It adjusts. It accounts for where you actually are, *not* where you "should" have been. And then it gives you a new way forward.

Calmly. Patiently. Without judgment.

It gives us more grace than we give ourselves.

Honesty and patience together create alignment.

Honesty without patience becomes harsh. Patience without honesty becomes avoidance. But together, they create alignment.

Honesty says, "This is where I am." Not where I wish I was. Not where I pretend to be. Not where others expect me to be. But where I actually am on the trail.

Patience says, "That's okay. Let's keep going." Not rushing. Not condemning. Not demanding an immediate overhaul. Just continuing with awareness.

Because sometimes you don't need to rebuild your whole life. You just need a small adjustment. A different step. A shifted perspective. A return to something simple you already know.

Becoming is not about perfection. It is about recalculating and recalibrating. Again and again. Over and over.

And when you learn to be both honest and patient with yourself, something beautiful happens. You stop fearing mistakes. You stop overreacting to missteps. You stop turning detours into identities.

You simply notice. You adjust. You stay on the trail.

The goal is never to walk the trail perfectly. The goal is simply to stay on the trail.

The Three Principles of the Trail to Becoming

1. You are never finished
2. You are never broken.
3. Always be honest and patient with yourself.

If you are struggling during your becoming process, I would bet money that one or all of these principles need attention and you've already identified which ones.

Now the challenge is simple and difficult at the same time. Get back on the trail. Find where you stepped off. And take that first step.

Keep moving. You are never finished. You are not broken. You are simply becoming.

About the Author
William "Scott" Faulkner

Scott Faulkner is an author, speaker, and mental health advocate whose life journey has been shaped by resilience, personal growth, and the pursuit of freedom beyond diagnosis.

A former state champion quarterback and defensive back at Titusville High School, Faulkner continued his athletic career as a defensive cornerback at Austin Peay State University, where he developed the discipline and determination that would later define his life's work.

Faulkner spent two decades as a property management professional before serving as a Physical Therapy Assistant in Florida for thirteen years. Following his retirement, he turned his attention to writing and public speaking, drawing from a lifetime of personal experience to help others overcome adversity.

Diagnosed with Bipolar Disorder in 1993, Faulkner spent much of his adult life navigating the challenges of mental illness, failed careers, broken relationships, and personal setbacks. Refusing to be defined by his diagnosis, he dedicated more than a decade to developing practical tools and strategies for personal transformation. Through programs such as The Elite Mindset™, Diagnosis Programming™, and The Walkabout™, he has empowered both himself and others to move from chaos and limitation toward lives marked by purpose, productivity, and freedom.

Now residing in Georgia, Faulkner continues to write, mentor, and speak publicly on the subject of *Living Beyond Diagnosis*. His second book, *The Grind of Living Beyond Diagnosis*, draws on lessons from football and life to address issues of identity, perseverance, and mental health, especially for men who often struggle to speak openly about their challenges.

Scott Faulkner is available for speaking engagements at colleges, churches, mental health organizations, military organizations, and athletic teams worldwide, where he shares a message of hope, resilience, and the power of living beyond limitations.

Contact William "Scott" Faulkner to share how this book has impacted you, for scheduling, or to place a bulk book order.

Email:livingbeyonddiagnosis65@gmail.com

Phone: 407-925-6616

STATE CHAMPION
16
S. Faulkner